AF597412

# *The Work of the Wrench*

*Other Books by Charles Edward Eaton*

*Poetry*
The Bright Plain
The Shadow of the Swimmer
The Greenhouse in the Garden
Countermoves
On the Edge of the Knife
The Man in the Green Chair
Colophon of the Rover
The Thing King

*Short Stories*
Write Me from Rio
The Girl from Ipanema
The Case of the Missing Photographs

*Critical Biography*
Karl Knaths: Five Decades of Painting

# *The Work of the Wrench*

Charles Edward Eaton

*Cornwall Books*
*New York • London • Toronto*

Cornwall Books
440 Forsgate Drive
Cranbury, NJ 08512

Cornwall Books
25 Sicilian Avenue
London WC1A 2QH, England

Cornwall Books
2133 Royal Windsor Drive
Unit 1
Mississauga, Ontario
Canada L5J 1K5

**Library of Congress Cataloging in Publication Data**

Eaton, Charles Edward, 1916–
The work of the wrench.

I. Title.
PS3509.A818W6 1985 811′.54 84-45452
ISBN 0-8453-4794-2

Printed in the United States of America

To Isabel

# *Contents*

# *Acknowledgments*

*Bennington Review* for permission to reprint "The Waltz" and "The Glyptograph."

*Boston Review:* "Suttee" and "Swimming Near the Interstate."

*California Quarterly:* "The Wetback" (under title, "On the Way to Sunset").

*College English:* "The Canal."

*Denver Quarterly:* "The Fan."

*The Georgia Review:* "Sand Hog" and "Two-Way Stretch."

*Grand Street:* "Slip of the Tongue."

*Hawaii Review:* "Nude Indigo" (under title, "Blue Nude").

*The Hollins Critic:* "Blue Streak" and "The Wrench."

*Kansas Quarterly:* "The Soft Spot" and "The Young Goat."

*The Kenyon Review:* "The Barge," "The Hammer Thrower," and "Blue Snapper Blues."

*Midwest Quarterly:* "The Image Exit" and "Witness for the Defense."

*Modern Poetry Studies:* "The Blue Hammer."

*Prairie Schooner:* "Text for the Flower Children."

*The Reporter:* "The Kite."

*Salmagundi:* "The Luck of the Zeppelin" and "Special Effects."

*Sewanee Review:* "After Degas" and "Cloud Pictures."

*Shenandoah:* "The Addict."

*South Carolina Review:* "Blue Grotto."

*Southern Humanities Review:* "The Barbarian."

*Southern Poetry Review:* "The Blood Paintings" and "The Plethora."

*The Southern Review:* "The Rickshaw."

*Tendril:* "The Uprising."

Acknowledgments are also due to the following magazines for permission to reprint one or more poems: *Blue Unicorn, Chouteau Review, Contact II, Cream City Review, Dalhousie Review* (Canada), *The Fiddlehead* (Canada), *International Poetry Review, Long Pond Review, Louisville Review, New Mexico Humanities Review, Pembroke Magazine, Poem, Red Clay Reader, San Jose Studies, The Smith, Webster Review,* and *West Coast Review.*

Also, "The Image Exit" was reprinted in the 1984 edition of the *Anthology of Magazine Verse and Yearbook of American Poetry* (Monitor Book Company).

"Writing Letters on a Train" was included in a special anthology issue of *Crosscurrents* (California), published in celebration of the XXIIIrd Olympiad in Los Angeles under the title "Literary Olympians: 1984."

"The Wrench" won the *Hollins Critic* Poetry Award for 1983.

# *The Work of the Wrench*

# I. *FOREIGN AFFAIRS*

## *THE BARGE*

The river was not much wider than an ordinary street,
Placid, waiting almost sexually to be penetrated:
The ferns, the flowers, somewhere not far off, the
maidenhead.

I had put aside my love for the great, white, luxurious ship,
The immense thrust of the blue crossing, the lights at night,
the dancing,
And committed myself to the beautiful, slow procedure of the
barge.

One could almost feel it taking long, graceful, deep steps in the
water
As it moved with precision through the prostrate legs of the
land,
The flowers like a ruffled, pulled-back skirt, the soft, soft ferns.

There was nothing like it—this coming on and being come
upon,
As if the brain were stroked two ways at once,
As though a metaphysical anxiety were almost put to rest.

We came in time to much more cluttered waters
Where the odor of water lilies shoved aside was overpowering
And the black nose of the boat seemed nearly pushed up in its
final nook.

We decided then and there to pause and stay the night—
Swung and locked in a hammock we seemed a single concept,
Thesis and antithesis borne and buried in the barge.

It was an impulse of origins and the stars sprinkled
A dust of silver on our languorous figures as if to warn us
That a mold of something else was always in the making.

We rose a little stiff for croissants, butter, honey
Which slid down in the mouth as if to keep us soft, forever sweet,
And the sun struck a mallet on our knees to make them flex.

We invaded, pushed, and pushed past the water lily glut
Much as one wipes away a thing too rich that clings and clings,
And the chin of the boat resumed its look of lazy, low bravado.

One scarcely remembers when or where the barge reached port,
How the old, handturned locks lifted us higher and higher, past flowers into the faces of people,
Or whether they smelled upon us the rut of the river.

I know this—the barge remains somewhere—in the jelly of the eye,
The rich intestinal canals, the heart's flowerlike clutch, the silt of the bone marrow—
We cannot join our hands but that the hammock sways.

## *THE WALTZ*

The room, so full of light and opulence,
Was humid and leafy as a forest,
The orchestra a clutch of cicadas,
Their thin, rasping legs bound in evening clothes—
The sun was hiding in a chandelier,
The threat of rain suspended in teardrops.
Or so it seemed when I came in to watch
Women's faces run like watercolor,
Leaving war paint on a dancing partner's cheek

Until he shook, shuddered down to a G string;
The cicadas gasped for a break in the music.
It was like Watteau toasted on a fire:
Some running to the washroom for safety,
Others drinking and drinking cold champagne,
A river, a boundary no flame could leap—
Just a moment before, an ecstasy:
The whirling, the hugging, kissing, a view
Of bobbing water lilies from the stairs—
Or so I was told by a beautiful girl
Who put her cool hand in mine like a present.
She had not danced, but stood back from the fire
To wait for Prince Charming in asbestos.
She did not know I brought the heavy tree
Glistening with fruit and dripping with moisture.
If anything, it hung above the ballroom,
Giving the enclosure its humid overplus.
Still we danced, the pictures dried themselves,
The cool brand of her hand upon my back.
The harsh grasshoppers turned to violins,
The G strings developed suspenders, pants,
A run in a violet stocking drank spit
And kept the fire from going up a skirt.
I tell this story of the hand and waltz
On hot summer days when the brain trickles
With a kind of rich, loose, forest weeping—
Even so one approaches the high blaze,
The music in constant metamorphosis,
The women laced, the men pressed almost naked,
The brief, wet tableau when the dancing stops.
Even now I am not detached from it:
My dreams have streaked, pink slippers in them,
The waterglass holds tepid champagne,
A grasshopper puts his bow to my chest,
My breached, damp clothes dangle the G string—
I roll over swaddled in waltz music:
The silver hand beats time against the wall.

## *THE TANK*

It rolls into the square as if it came to drink,
Tipped up like a whale beside the fountain:
A bewildered peasant woman stands nearby, watering the tank.

That's only the first image with which the heart is torn.
We so longed for the relative purity of *détente*
The monstrous, protrusive gun endows a sorely encrusted
  unicorn.

But where is the virgin slated for his capture?
The prostitutes already look as though they feared shaved
  heads
For having given to their own countrymen one moment of sad
  rapture.

Kept fishlike in the mind, it must be allowed to slide,
Heavy-scaled, subaqueously phallic, pushing at the maidenhead
Of the great, submerged, prostrate form of ancient pride.

But the lumbering thing has other ways of making sense.
We have put it together to come and graze upon us,
And now, sitting down across the street, we think to stop it with
  a human fence.

Slumped from the fabulous head, the horn moves slowly
  round, an exhibitionist's crotch—
The woman screams, finding the fountain suckled dry,
And a child comes up to try his pacifying touch.

## *THE UPRISING*

That rich field of poppies and then the plow,
The long, bloodied furrows of crushed flowers—
Pleasure was a possession that belonged
To him to be turned over when he willed.

At one end of the field, a coifed haystack
Reminded him of harvested women,
Last year's lovers grown gray in sun and wind,
Heaped where another poppy field was turned.

Some such sensation of full-blown summer
Makes a ruthless prince of ordinary men,
The black boot on a clump mashed with flowers,
All those transformations whirled in a wig.

Next, one must summon the keenest harrow,
Over and over the complaisant clods,
Until it can pour a silt of rubies,
Dust to mix in wax for a red shoeshine.

The tall man in black, the sprinkled oxford—
How do these images of ourselves arise?
Why cannot we put hasps upon the book
Of pleasure, the safe and pristine poppy?

An ordinary man sleeps nude in red socks,
That much memory of life's rare conquest,
As if he waded through dreams in the deep blood's
Ground water, a long ditch of disclosure.

Comes simplistic morning and he must slice
An apple in the kitchen for breakfast,
Devour a bowl of cherries with white teeth
That grind the pits like gravel of the field.

Perhaps he will take the day off and spend it
In the hayloft smelling the seed of sex
To the point of vertigo, the sneeze, the cough,
His nerves a hachure of those poppy fields.

One of our ancient icons, the peasant,
Trousers open, lying under the stack,
Dreams of the girl in the flowered skirt,
Clutched, trammeled like a bunch of blossoms.

One takes the long way round through history

En route to poppies in tight buttonholes,
The crosses like tines of dismantled harrows,
The shaved heads of prostitutes grown thick again.

When I trust my foot to the small bootblack,
The sunlight winks a ruby in his eye—
A young girl in red passing in the street
Smiles, gives her revolutionary stare.

## *BLUE GROTTO*

There is something in graffiti that provokes
The deep-sea cave with its dark blue water,
As if the veins must transfer their thick lode
Into a place only roughly contained,
Neither ablution nor absolution
Wanted—just the rock back and forth of blue:
The nude drawing, the infinite paint pot,
The full underground luxury of means.

This is surely better than the ghetto
Which lies on the land like an open sore:
Blue figures mingle, drain in the sewers,
The eternal gravamen, their icon—
There is no one to loose, to lance, to let
The drawn ecstasy wander off the walls,
Push seaward, find its own cove, fill the rocks,
Carry with it its own voluptuous frieze,
The kept, debouched decalcomania.

The crude effort may underlie indeed
The great wall paintings of the past, the grace
That stretches the dance far along the road
As if the pulled wave knew no rude pinchback—
One will go richly wreathed, at last, somehow:
I have seen women lift it in my face,

The hand that blooms in the rounded picture,
A blue bag, groped, and heavy with the sea—
An ease, an outlet, swinging on their arms.

## *THE RICKSHAW*

He had not meant to visit this exotic land,
Or fall in love, at least so soon, but there she was,
And someone like himself was pulling them by hand.

He did not like to ride on just two wheels, beneath a hood,
The harnessed human being, also in the driver's seat,
This sturdy, compact man who concentrated on the thing he
   understood.

But there were parasols, kimonos, everywhere,
A girandole of images through which he ran—
Excited, singed with doubt, he had become somehow divided
   there.

His sweet companion offered porcelain and painted lip,
A plaintive and endearing piece of man-drawn baggage
Who paused upon the paper and would not raise the whip.

He forced the line and brought it down himself upon his
   back—
Those who find themselves somewhere they had not meant to
   be
Know how far it reaches from the self, the stinging line that
   takes up all your slack.

I used to look at pictures of rickshaw runners as a child—
Something must have told me even then of faultless figurines,
   the rolling frenzy
Where vivid streets hallucinate the startled word, the
   double-entendre running wild.

## *THE LUCK OF THE ZEPPELIN*

The dirigible was like a floating nude,
The cloud-tufted blue sky her great divan—
In the light, from silver to damascene,
Sliding tints on a woman's sleek thighs.

So love looks tethered there for a moment,
The fabulous, elongate, opaque bubble
Scanning the mountain's puncturing purple peak,
The sea's decuman lifting its lavish tongue.

Thus do we dream to start the lover's day,
Immense, moored, still but pregnant with journeys.
Can we not at least indulge ourselves at dawn
With life's loveliest, elated languor?

Ah, comes the scented wind, the slightest puff
That questions our control as if, after all,
No virgin but a demimondaine stirs,
Welcoming many from those foreign lands.

Jazz blares from the pendent cabin—One thinks
Of the necklaced women, the spatted men
Uncluttered by commitment or belief
As if always high and tuned for evening.

The skin of the balloon now sweats champagne—
You can imagine the monocled captain
With a side interest in the white slave trade
Stumped in his puzzle by the one word Love.

If we do not yell the answer from below,
He will give command to sail without us,
And the woman we did not know was ruined
Will not even leave a short goodbye note.

Over the Atlantic in deepest night
One turns to the girl beside one

As if she wore waterwings forever,
The safe, soft breasts of the born stowaway.

Cocooned in the corrupt oval, one floats—
Jazz in the saloon, the diddling captain,
Free of the mountain's finger, the lush mouth
Of the sea. Nothing but us is moving.

This is what we tell ourselves about sex:
Metaphysics stopped by inflated walls,
Magic lanterns surrounding us with lights,
Intense, exquisite, stationary pictures.

I recall blowing bubbles as a child,
How they lit like exploded butterflies—
One lives with wiped, iridescent fingers,
Launching every morning with another ship.

## *THE PEOPLE PACKAGE TOUR*

Some days you cannot move the world a jot—
You stand impacted but want brilliantly to spread out,
Release the tube of color that lies behind the spot.

You feel like water that cannot saturate as rain:
The full, distended look, but nothing bleeds—
Even a sensual hand would come away from you without
  apparent stain.

When everyone around you is shifting ground,
Their travels like a mist from squirting tubes,
You are staked forever, that enamel figure on his sacrificial
  mound.

Islands of purple, out there, beyond, anywhere you turn—
If someone else has taken over every haunting place,

There is nothing to do with these white faggots but let them burn.

Perhaps just smoke at first, and then pink steam—
I have seen the white man burning when the others leave
As if to signal all the tribes to light their fires and dream.

Huge pink and pluming flowers as the figures in the forest twist—
Those who return with bits of ivory, whitest lace, vapid in an hour,
Come to be known in this stark place as Little People of the Mist.

## *IGLOO*

When something hardens in the pleasure dome,
We build the igloo, a certain icing
In the orange, a flower turning to glass,
Spangles on a skirt dripping icicles.

One tried puttees even in the tropics—
Constriction merely invited the cold
As though that winding snake of cloth wanted
To make a caduceus of the torso.

Blue skies, velvet dusks were milked for glamor
Until the nightcap tasted like bluejohn;
We soaked our underwear in jasmine oil
As if that would protect us from frostbite.

Surely the waterfall with the brown girls
Swimming below would remain our ladder
As we stretched out naked in the warm sun,
Poaching our hearts with the souls of salmon.

The golden crests of palms falling like nets,
The bright fish, caught live, so soon enameled—
A last girl stood on the lip of the pool,
Having drunk a chilled solution from stone.

Must we countenance this dispossession?—
The sun disk, a trophy in the living room,
Replaced with the head of an arctic beast,
The rich carpet growing claws and a snout.

Packed with men, meat, and fur, indehiscent,
The igloo answers the diamond in the heart.
Just this—the flaw of blood sleeps then glitters,
Growing tumid as it trues its dome.

## *THE IMAGE EXIT*

The tunnel through the mountain suggested terrifying
power —
The dentist's drill, the auger, the little boring-in, the immense
contained, ruthless operation—
And right at the tunnel mouth the exquisite quaresma tree in
purple flower.

The dentist may not let you go so easily again;
The engineer's crude ambition is absolutely endless:
The dentist smiles, quaresma offers you, for terror, this purple
ruff around your pain.

So urban, tropic, images make their radical and rueful blend—
Aided by narcotics, I sat in the chair dreaming
Of how the mind kept thinking of the blossom, the tunnel that
would never end.

It does though in an enormous sucked-through flower of sun—

Browbeaten by the light, you are as well bedizened:
Vision comes back, almost as heavy as flung jewels, to the
propelled and punctured one.

Caves as compared with cavities, the elevator and the rising
chair—
Were you told in a trance of the existence of a secret gold mine,
Vertical or horizontal—then shafted, shafted, without knowing
where?

It has been years and years and years since I was there—the
ultra South—
Many chairs, tunnels—*exeunt omnes*—the blinding nimbus just a
bit too large to wear:
The dentist smiles, the open face of rock has a purple stain
around the mouth.

## *THE HAMMER THROWER*

One wants some gold paint, oil for enfleurage,
The flowers leaching their pervasive smell,
A spattered, highly scented mixing-place—
Of course it would be better if sunlight
Gilded the nude in the studio corner,
The crushed flowers were released from bondage,
Or so we are told—but who believes it?
The floor is strewn with our exuviae:
A last year's flaking of our summer tan,
The dashed rose like a stepped-on, greaseless kiss,
A flung bottle, the faint, nostalgic scent—
It may not look it, but this was meant to be
A place of projection, the white nude seen
As something painted gold and powerful,
A perfume pouring from a hero's mouth
Into the dark caves of halitosis
Where the lion waits with a thorn in his foot—

Summer has no keener light and odor
Than these mixing-places of our choosing,
A secret skylight winking at the heart,
The miasma lurking in tight-lipped books.
One wishes to dip the peach in metal,
Fatten it to be thrown like a hammer,
The released athlete whirling in a scent,
Our brilliant dervish, the earth's gyroscope—
Someone at last finds the delved, golden ball,
The far, blind reach of an enthrottlement,
An expelled gorge of the full swallowed day.
I like to walk in fields and meadows,
Dreaming of flash, rush, whirr, the manic shower,
Feeling the rounded rock beneath the arch
As the giant deals with the lodged pebble—
I have come to the end of paving stones,
The unstirred sunlight, the fulsome flowers.

# II. *INCIDENCE OF ORMOLU*

## *THE BARBARIAN*

Having eaten the torso of a pear,
Another full, ripe, beheaded body
For breakfast, the barbarian looked out
And saw the Northern fog still huddled there,
Unaccommodating to all totems
As if God's mind poisoned the stagnant air—
Hadn't he spit out the seeds in a kind
Of sowing, left the woman herself in bed?
What did the world want from these small pleasures?—
That the pear itself should drool its anguish,
Casting him in the role of a dragon?
Why did the stream call to his lips for scum?
He only wanted something on the side:
The pear, voluptuous idol on the table,
An ecstatic rush of sweetness in the mouth
While the woman dreamt of the stone goddess
Which dominated their days together—
That cannibalism, a thing so small—
One switches this on, only now and then,
As if it were a rude, recessed, kept altar,
The sacrificial blood the juice of pears—
One speaks softly then, wakens the woman,
Brushing the marble from her stalled body.
I have seen this man with his storm cellar
Full of fruit stand at his own bland mirror,
Remembering the stirred pond's unhealthy smell,
His blue eyes skating on the silver skin—
Something one will remember forever:
How little, lurking pleasures always live

With the pear's abdomen in their rough hands—
I can feel that figure even in the mist.

## *WILD GOOSE CHASE*

They thought he was dead, humped up, both soft and hard—
It was as though random life had all these feathers left over
And, for want of something better to do, stuffed them with
frozen lard.

He is just an appearance now whose disappearance perhaps
belonged to the gun.
We come in and go out so casually—a final arrested image
Only so long as it takes a rank, feathered pudding to rot in the
sun.

I seem to stand by the supposed corpse completely instilled:
What seems to be stays as it is. All we can do
Is say to the dead: With gold, these wounds of mine are filled—

Much as a white, rotten tooth is by the metal lined
And takes bold issue with the crammed, abdicating mouth:
I throw the brilliant gleam of an eye into a room while you
plead blind.

It is the strangest thing—this mixing of teeth, gold, and
feathered grease—
Something is beating on my mind these days with such fantastic
force
That I shall soon be asking Lazarus: How does one resurrect
these geese?

One bites a bit metallic, and look—the lard is living goose—
Lean with the loaded scar, body-length, livid with gold, into a
lump of life,
And all our concepts with their percepts may be up and
running, wild and loose.

# *CARCANET*

How did the iron become so bedizened,
His blond head bulging like a Roman melon,
His flaccid body, an old, plump rag doll?—
Nothing at first but garroting metal
As though the hands of history had melded,
The thick, glistening flies their only jewels—
Did he simply slowly ripen in place,
The light brushing his face with carotene,
Roughening it a bit like canteloupe,
Tethered forever as if he were the sun's dog?
Who bred this amalgam of mush and metal,
The over-mellow head longing to fall,
The tongue dripping its foolish, salt diamonds?—
One has many fantasies, but this one
Cannot be measured by the mind's calipers.
Some day you are simply put there in place,
The unadorned rim in hard remembrance.
Your eyes will graze over the green meadows
While the head keeps softening in the sun
And the veins run outward like catheters—
Just that bloated protuberance of sensation
Choked upward by a long runaway life.
Someone at last brings you a drink of water,
This indeed your very finest lover,
And some silver spills on the black circlet.
You are on your way to magnificence—
Perhaps another brings you a bowl of cherries
And the sun picks up the tab for vermeil.
The chin would let down fine gold catenas
As a beard if given encouragement.
One can hardly otherwise explain
How a thing worn so long becomes adorned
As if montage comes home to the mountain.
The next time a collar squeezes you too tight,
Leaving green and black torque-marks on the flesh,
Be bold, wink a ruby on it right away,
Knowing how the bloodshot eye can spare it
And the stuck vein purples up its sapphire.

Oh, the fields and fields of fallen faces
With their ripe, rouged cheeks and long gashed lips,
The stuffed and headless scarecrows wandering!—
I see a necklace lying in a chair
As if a certain weight cannot wither,
My hand at my throat for rainbow splotches
As though I felt those fingers with their flies.

## *THE CANAL*

Sometimes it seemed like an enormous magnification of a vein
Stretched outside his room where his heart still beat without it,
Filled with debris and slime, the circulation almost slowed to a
   halt.

He felt a little like an animal that soiled itself
Every time he threw down a cigarette butt, a paper cup, a
   rotten fruit.
How far would they move from him in such slow pulse?

Only the youngest and most vital men live easy by a sluggish
   water,
Those who recirculate the world each night twice over in their
   dreams,
Whom even the vampire cannot drain of the will to live.

Still, he was left in this large, once grand, and rotting place,
An old magnifico, his hands grabbing at the rumpled sheets
Like mattocks digging pictures in this lifted, secret garden.

How did the red and rushing stream become at last this
   menacing canal
With its sweetish, sickish smell of sangria fermenting
As if the simple scuppernong had had too long a ride along the
   river?

Was nothing left to him but the fishmonger down below,

Fat as a manatee, crying up the freshness of the red slit throats
As he failed to dig up at dawn a buried, shimmering woman on
a shell?

Shall I tell him what I recommend, having left a dozen cities
with their old canals,
Not minding a silver-buckled belt left behind, a mouth syringe,
If a single brilliant, brought-up picture frees the thrombus
from another day?

In suchwise one walks the world somewhat like a shining
postcard,
A demonstrator, if you will, of how one wins the water strike,
Stopping the traffic with a hand holding up the likeness of a
Venus.

I thought this out one day in a very old, run-down hotel—
If not one day, then another, visions of slimy false teeth in a
glass
Competing with spiders of sunlight and shadow crawling in so
many directions.

I do not insist too much—one cannot always do it—
No archeologist who lies too long, too late, too stiff in bed
Can rouse the chambermaid Veronica to wipe a moving picture
from his face.

## *THE GIMLET*

The stark, brilliant, sea light singeing his eyes,
The heart made jealous by the swollen fruit—
It is one of those mythical days when you
Have come to spread mica on the asphalt

Like the final touch of false diamonds
Or scales from the hard eye of a lizard—

Last night women rhumbaed on the dance floor
Under the trees and left a scum of sequins.

One tries to trap pool water in the eyes,
Backed up under the caves of the eyelids;
The heart is well wrapped in a flowered shirt,
Camouflaged against the threat of suntan:

Who wants a sun-cured mango in his chest?—
This conjectured of a man who has not been
To the tropics in so many years
But nevertheless has a sliding scab

Of brilliance looking for a place to stick—
One considers constantly the mind, how
It hides its sores against all healing,
Picks at the festering would-be jewels:

The sting and thrill of that thick, salt, blue wave,
The hope of being stunned by a coconut
As if a crown awry were better than none,
The foot longing for the merde of mangoes.

At least one can sweep up the dance floor
Into an enormous haystack of sequins
Like the hated harvest of happiness—
That last deep kiss with its third degree burn.

Will the scab now settle its solitaire?—
Even a big glass-bottomed boat will do,
Enough to see the entrails of the sea plants,
Those weaving, waving, and imploring weeds.

This is what makes the lover's hand so rare—
The diamond, a tombstone, but no coffin—
As if in its small focus it caught
Or simply waited for a drop of blood.

And so we withhold the nail, the gimlet,
Spend a lifetime in the sleek glissade—

Yes, yes, indeed, the loose pox of glitter,
The spotted fever licking at its glue.

## *THE BLOOD PAINTINGS*

How could he tell them of his picture-haunted days
When the voluptuous cherries in the white porcelain dish
Seemed to be the only thing worth having in the world?

How could they know he did not mind the rich monotony,
Reinvesting the moment over and over as if he poured slowly
The implacable silt of his inordinate attention?

It is the difference between the once-for-all, gashed-throat
approach,
And the drop-by-drop, nails in the hands, so that the
punctured veins
Learn the patient, healing power of the stalactite.

Perhaps, after all, he wanted nothing more than this:
To build up a picture of impassioned preference
As a red tear sits and swells upon another.

For one must never leave out some sadness,
The fatigue of the vein, milked and milked once too often,
A sense that the roof can weep no more.

Therefore, the frame of the simplest picture is a cavern,
Or so I wanted to tell the man, dropping, dropping down his
blood,
To say that someone saw the ogive and the niche.

No wonder the old masters loved grottoes and recesses,
Knowing how full of moss and ferns repeated passion is—
The man will sit there until the cherries are the swollen tears of
Christ.

That, as we say, is the background of the picture—
Later, the man and I ate the cherries with much pleasure,
And left the white dish there to catch the droppings from the
sky.

We agreed to picture ourselves again and again,
The damp days and the dry days underneath the endless
arches,
The many-colored tear secreted in the rich arrested fruit.

## *SUTTEE*

Picture a jeweled woman by the fire
Who has come with her bedizened memory:
That ring given when her first child was born—
Bracelets, necklaces, heavy padlocks,
And no one now but him could find the keys.
She had walked so long in the blazing sun,
A flush, open casket, but hands cannot
Steal from the soft cushion of her skin.

There in the hot fire, the roast of the past,
A brass smell of flesh wanting to be timeless—
One imagines the heart beating a gong
For the man of bronze who will drip no fat,
A pyre somewhere by every human hutch:
All over the world, the women in silk,
The outdoor barbecue, the men with meat
Watching the smoke in some far, marble place.

Then comes the time to set oneself alight—
Can one do it for this brown, soot-smudged man
With his loose belt, no cummerbund, no keys?
Ah, those smoky, sensuous, summer evenings—
I have seen her hesitate, palm the match,
Then light a cigarette. Shish kebab drips,

The fire flares—jewels flashing everywhere
Look like eyes, embers, scattered from a box.

## *THE MYTH IN THE MODULE*

It may not rouse the world, subject to stronger shocks,
To see a large, red-faced man without obvious purpose
Standing in a magnificent garden, fingering white phlox.

But I am rather drawn to what this duo, misallied, can mean.
I am enamored of the far-fetched and absurd,
And keep my images on a pad, ready for the launching scene.

I study that furrowed, pocked face, saturnine—from what red
wars?
He holds a scepter in his hand as if appealing to the faith
That I can send him as the only king we have, roaring off to
Mars.

I can do much for him, but, sirrah, sirrah, I cannot do that—
At this point, he flatly cools to terra cotta taciturn,
And all the candid clustered diamonds in the phlox are matte.

I have seen this happen rather often in the garden:
Some potentially propulsive, even violent, pair, turned to a
far-off realm,
Will not quite get off the launching pad, but fizzle, simmer,
harden.

I am left with a rigid flower, incomparable cabal, the canceled
man of clay.
Everything is loaded, irremissible—"All systems Go!"—
And I, or the man who would be king, abort for another day.

## *THE FOSSIL*

When the warm hand he lay on went to sleep,
He thought, this is the touch of the fossil,
The numb feeling before stone takes over,
The thick leaf of flesh mineralizing,
So many autumns in the underground—
Then the whole plant of the body silting,
The last desire calling for gold at least,
The groin hardening like a daffodil bulb,
The tight flower, metallic, introverted—
One can imagine the last words silvering
Underneath the rigid bubble of breath,
A geodesic dome over language.
Most of all, the veins reverse, rushing back
To the full ruby fortress of the heart
Only to find rock thinking of the ages,
Aloof as a mesa to its rivers—
Nothing in the world weeps but stalactites:
Around the caves—the skeletons, leaves, flowers.
At this point, he stirs beneath the crust, rubs
As if he used a ghost for his massage.
Even in his stupor he feels a vein
Struggling to clear out the plaque, ream its lode.
Some few words warm to a thick morning mist,
Desire remembers Proserpina's hand,
A trumpet longs to blare from the stiff loins;
The fossorial grasp shudders his nerves full-length—
In an old world to delve in, he will dig
The remains once more, the five-fingered leaf,
The heavy body still hung with mineral meat,
Himself again, and all he knows of earth.

# *MONTAGE FOR MARTINETS*

Each day the blood requires an acrobatic stunt—
The vivid pictures in the brain compete like tumblers:
One hazards a rajah's jeweled turban, one hopes for a tiger
  hunt.

Nothing is beyond this wavering arabesque—
One thinks to keep the head in reach, wearing just a baseball
  cap,
But one among those bold and naked figures ends up in a
  casque.

So we afflict ourselves with all that we can take of regimental
  drill,
Nude soldiers sounding off, counting off forever,
But somewhere in high grass the members of the raj are
  hunting still.

I am too white, too nude, and long for darker skin,
Hot eyes, oil, unction, the warmest wealth of jewels:
I am being made by those stark figures illiterate within.

Which is not to say that anything but art can tap
What is of the world but not yet in it,
Heating to explosion whole gymnasiums underneath a baseball
  cap.

Just when we have them in a row, something rigid slips—
"Wipe that smile off your face" could be received in Sanskrit:
From man to man one cannot say who thinks himself the rajah
  with the reddest lips.

# *THE CARBUNCLE*

The swimmer, not yet tanned, somewhat turned toward age,
With the pustulating carbuncle on his arm,
Would seem this side of any charm,
Leprous, illuminated to himself, upon a medieval page.

Must we in middle age turn cruel
To ourselves, to others, when the pin
Point swells beneath unblemished skin,
A sore that has a name in common with a jewel?

So much is concentrating now, so much is done—
We have been lavish, even lewd,
Done everything that you can do as nude,
And now must wear this garish oval in the sun.

The brilliant skin will never be the same—
Some might even see the bosses of the chest,
Ambiguous these days, not altogether blest:
Thank God, we share, in part, the jewel-name.

So we must learn to lance these garnets
As if we ran a rapid jeweler's concern,
Taking in the spunk and spoils of every stress in turn—
We lose some flaws perhaps, knowing how to cut the stone just
before it sets.

# *INCIDENCE OF ORMOLU*

With his great stolid life, the man was nevertheless a passionate dreamer,
Not night dreams, though they were freer, but, in the end, without effect:
He wanted a dream that bloomed or bulged in the light of day.

It must put a pool, like the largest sapphire in the world, beside the house—
A garden of such intricate beauty that everyone gasped;
A collection of art that rivaled that of a monarch.

He was such a solid man, heavily muscled, a bronze,
In fact, if he could only have been satisfied with that:
To have one incomparable, indisputable treasure—a mind and body made of bronze.

But he much preferred to think of himself, in extremis, packed with these fabulous dreams,
And sometimes wished that he had a stained glass window in his side
So that the enthusiasts for bronze could see what glowed in among the meshes.

He could spend a whole day just forming, fondling, the sapphire,
Another day on his hands and knees planting exotic species in the botanical garden,
A whole week going through the galleries of the world.

And all the time to his friends he remained an object, better still, an *objet,*
A bronze artifact they would gladly have put in the corner
Of some flat and airless room, safe from pigeons, verdigris, safe from everything.

Thus we may be once and forever placed by those who do not know us:

Everyone a bronze to someone, more or less idealized, more or less grotesque,
But a great ponderous weight at the end of a room where no one dreams.

So much, then, for the pool, pictures, the garden richer than Eden—
The man was a solid citizen who held down a corner of the house—
All that one wished for him were days without end and a mantle of dust.

# III. *THE MISCHIEF IN THE MIRROR*

## *BLUE STREAK*

In the luminous shade of the hotel
The man waited for the thrust of the day.
It was not enough to eat crescent rolls,
Feel the jam in his teeth like luscious grit.
There in his great sonorous loneliness
He would have been glad for the brilliant sun
To have reduced itself into a ball
Rolled in the room like a yellow billiard,
Smoking up the silver of the mirror
As if made ready for total eclipse,
Parting his thick, black hair with brilliantine,
Burning a cicatrice across his scalp,
The swift, round, smooth, and voluble entry—
Lacking that, take up the binoculars,
Watch the sea making its blue advances,
A wet mouth full of erotic language.
Imagine a magnet in the lenses
To pick up those gold nudes locked in embrace,
The windy palm trees sucked up like thistles,
The glistening sand, chips of a solitaire.
Keep looking until one feels beauty spots
Where the rims of the binoculars touch,
Lids and cheekbones pressed with white eye shadow
As if those who see too much turn savage.
It is this combination of desire—
To feed and feed yet keep a gentle heart—
That makes the eye pull the lighthouse down
Like a stick of sugar in blue water.
No wonder we sometimes talk a blue streak

When found alone in an invaded room:
What it was like to feel sun through your hair,
The flaked gold that lovers leave on the lids.

## *WRITING LETTERS ON A TRAIN*

Summer is out there somewhere, the flowers, fruit, sea,
  sun—and youth.
We have drunk too much, bitten too bitter and too deep,
  smelled the scent of flesh:
Why must our companion traveling in the mirror be so
  addicted to the truth?

Not silver, though dusk bequeaths it, certainly not morning
  gold—
The suitcase full of handsome clothes sags impossibly with lead
As if it were the only metal that could mount the mirror that
  we hold.

But the old magnificence, the makings are still there—
All the gold that I would ever need is in the next compartment
Where a girl is brushing out the glorious metal of her hair.

I write a letter and the ink I spill—just one fat drop—
Begs never to be blotted but to lie serenely sure
Until it can be added to the sea—our inevitable next stop.

The train jolts, a light that plays along my pen
Seems to travel without mercy deep into the brain,
Quivers, enlarges, like a javelin some sorceress has thrown.

Such tears as if an ocean ruptured, such flowers, fruit, and
  sun—
When I recovered from that sorcery, I broke the pen in two,
As though the head of a lance should finish the letter just
  begun.

# *THE STREAMSIDE RESTAURANT*

In the streamside restaurant I could dream forever—
Had I eaten enough fruit, did the last heavy, ripe peach
Prepare me for the foundry? Was I ready for bronze?

These late years I could be cast in a single pose of pleasure:
The grape at the lip wanting to be swallowed,
The eye aglow with the sight of a lovely girl.

Someone has planted a penny at the base of my retina—
I want the image to pause and consider its life,
The pear come face to face with its own bas-relief—

The grape feeling a pressure of wine in the pulp
When it reaches the hard edge of its potential,
The tear admitted as a kind of pristine distillation.

This is what we do with the soft and hard of things—
This incurable devouring until the end of life,
The wanting to bite down upon the golden pit like gravel of a
   graded experience.

Just when one thinks one has simplified—another restaurant,
   another luscious meal—
This time for sure the overlooked white pearl in the oyster
As if, long in the tooth, we need once more enameling.

I should not have drunk that last glass of wine, eaten the torte,
But I want to go down the rippling stream well laden
If I should bump, like the ferry, against the always unexpected
   landing.

It is the feeling, indeed the hope, there will be resistance
   downstream,
The fovea centralis projecting its own keen copper,
That makes us forever cultivate the buffer in the nerves.

Therefore, neighboring towns can wait. The woman goes by
With her melon-headed baby in a carriage, and one loves the
notion
That he thumps his head against the very softest cushions.

I wonder if they did not profoundly know in the old walled
towns
Of this excess—that we must draw the line somewhere
And still let the huge vein of the stream move on, go down.

They raised some astounding figures always in the square—
These late years something still reminds us of them, the
pigeons, the acid,
As we pay the waiter and, on impulse, tip him far too
handsomely.

Why not?—The beautiful reversal has set in. I reconsider the
image,
How it drops its exquisite weight and goes, the peach, the
grape, the lovely girl,
My body laden with invisible cameos. Why should I ever want
to leave?

## *WHY THE SEA LOVES THE FIRE*

The man in the blue robe by the fireplace
Lately fleshes his dreams with mermaids,
Soft pink smudges in the drifting gray mist,
Auroral then draining off in pink suds
With his hands clearly missing a handful—
I do not know what one can do with a fiction
But let it glow, gleam, disintegrate,
Waking in bed with the streaked, strained feeling,
The heart a sieve with some clinkers in it,
Pink cabochons congealed from a mermaid
As if birthmarks were stone-deep in her flesh.

Still, not quite—more than a rattle of gravel,
More than plaque along a pink river
As you lift the day with locks to sea level.
Now by the fire, a box of fragrant cigars
At his side, roughly robed like a bluefish,
Considering his part of the baited world,
The man will let the pink mermaid surface,
No blood on the mouth, no dangling metal,
Just glowing breasts and long sequined tail.
Such liaisons are legumes of the sea;
They grow at the very quivering end
Of the tensions of the day, are pulled in
As you beach yourself in the long, blue robe,
The room no more than a place of driftwood,
The clank of keys in pockets, so many hooks.
The first drink tastes like sea air, swabbed, swizzled—
I have banked it too often with these men
Not to know how evenings connect themselves,
That the fire laid somehow fathoms the dream,
And morning leaves its stigmas in the hand.

## *HACIENDA*

Hung with purple bougainvillea, the walls washed white,
The hacienda obsesses me as the place not found:
It comes and goes as in the soul's most vacillating light.

The picture floats with extraordinary joy and shoots with
pain—
Someone is beating horseshoes on an anvil, someone is picking
fruit:
I am there, I have been there often, and I will not come again.

Where is that dusty case, and those binoculars?—
I can see the drunken cowboy leering from the barn,
Someone has picked my heart of strings for those guitars.

The summoned scent of all the flowers never lies—
It is as though some wayward woman sprayed this aura in a room
And I were kneeling at her feet to plead: I breathe, I breathe—you atomize.

Which is not to say in some other guise it will not surface—
The luck of the Bougainvilles changes, waxes, wanes,
And saturated, scented, sotted, I will look forever for the great good place.

I may be with you in the mountains, by the sea, but any moment will repair
To something like that white, low-slung house wreathed in purple,
And will not mind if you should call a great distraction my hacienda stare.

## *HELIOGRAPH*

The day your heart is in your mouth I will
Send you my message from the sun: Take off
The hairshirt and a harem will blossom
Near the courtyard—the eunuch will loosen
His hammerlock when the mirror flashes.
I will lay a sword of light at your feet.
There will be ripe fruit and Turkish candy,
The fountain cleansed of infusoria,
Oil on the hinges when the courtesans
Come through the great door—These are my signals.
If you wish, go on living hand to mouth,
Taking a thrown-down pit instead of the peach,
Letting the sweet turn acid on the tongue,
The untouched girl drop her oleograph,
Your answer to the message of desire—
I cannot flash this, off and on, too long;

I feel a gorge also rising hourly,
A dark eye in my hand at any moment.
Two legs falter, long for the tripod;
I will leave the mirror stuck in a frame—
While there is still time, go to the hangar,
Release the revved-up bird of paradise,
Take the fairest from the bearded Sultan:
I can imagine your let-down in a dream.
Believe me, it is better than ouija,
This tapping of the meaning of the sun.
If I burn a red sore place on your arm,
Forgive, for once, the misdirected aim.
I have these many patches from my lovers,
The skin's lost harlequin of happiness.
Remember instead how oblique I let
The eye see the Word in the lissom air,
The place where the fountain fuses in code,
The rainbow the houri picks up in her veils.

## *DISCS*

So much sun and pleasure, and then this small black spot—
I sat like a soft statue in the crowded absence of light,
And had some second thoughts about what I could do, what
  not.

The great spotlight which completely encircled the earth gone
  dim—
Outside, beyond, for millions and millions of miles there was
  light:
I sat in nothing but shadow, and it had a hardened rim.

One had an utterly new notion of position and part—
Here in the tondo of darkness one felt like an embryo,
And, for the life of him, who could detect the head, the tail, the
  heart?

All of this—just think of it!—through lack of pleasure and sun:
Carved from a domino without the galaxy of spots,
You long to ask the brilliant child of yesterday: Am I, or you, the one?

At this point, something in you, after all an embryo of noon,
Sees a hand, and then an arm, detached, lying in the sun:
A soft sensation, something coming in, something going out, enlarging or deflating the balloon.

Now light again, earth-wide, a brilliant mirror meant to flatter—
Shall I ever rid myself of this impassioned focus, all, or almost nothing:
An *ingénu* at large—the child of dark, the much too close placental matter?

## *THE HALCYON*

Perhaps we long for it most on sleepless nights,
The alert, startling conception drifting
Seaward toward the nest of the halcyon
Built up of blue twigs, mortared with sea foam.

One wants above all else to be that bird,
Make love, breed in a place of peace and calm,
To find the one glamourous, lost health-spot
Where the sea is soft as a woman's breast.

Voices outside your room are like sharp chalk
Drawn on a blackboard, the milkman stumbles
And spills splintered galaxies of white blood;
From his finial, the crow envies that far haunt.

The bed you lie on feels full of coarse twine
And horsehair, the work of your inland hours;

Lumps in the mattress are the semi-soft eggs
Of loosely connected indecisions.

While the heart gurgles like a failed embryo,
Not one thought seems to have broken its shell
Cleanly, sat proudly on a seat of blue—
It is much, much too soon for the phoenix.

One must first have had the rich, brilliant life
Which dies into itself like finished sex,
Eyes opening again with tiny feathers,
The whole bright body bristling and burning.

The sire of the phoenix is the halcyon—
One can never not have seen the floating nest—
Like an oasis on one's own stretched skin,
Blue, white, gleaming—and later strike the match.

Cultivate, therefore, those halcyon hours
That heal the leper with his own best spots.
Life loves the spreading skin transplant that takes—
The extended archipelago of nests.

I can feel it sliding on me some days,
The ecstatic, charmed, erogenous zone—
What does it matter if the living disc
Moves like a foreign body on its own?

## *KAYAK*

Does the handsome man in the kayak have a lover
Or live a little sad, paddling solo in the water,
Prepared, of course, eminently prepared, but not caring
  whether he turns over?

Does he have dreams of that gracious, open, green canoe

With a sumptuous cushion where a beautiful woman can lean back,
A moving, glorious, little world obviously built for two?

Those animal skins, snug, stretched tautly to his hips
Simplify his life: one man, one life, one lode,
So far removed from that delicious, but entangling world of arms and lips.

The day is lovely, the destination certain, the water, lucid, matte,
There is no white seductive hand dawdling in its own reflection,
No dangerous Mata Hari of the place beneath the picture hat.

No one to spy upon the nearly, but not quite, solipsistic world—
The mind cuts the water as though it opened a letter to itself,
The white birds fly over like a private flag unfurled.

Then why does he go suddenly mad, flip sideways-somersault, surrender
The causerie with calm, the white, immaculate banner of the birds,
Over and over, as if the arms of the Lady of the Lake turned him in a blender?

## *THE WETBACK*

Looking at a vein one dreams the wetback,
And playing chess you think of Harlequin
As if one moved counters on one's own skin—
The zither of nerves longs for the plectrum,
A xylophone deep-buried in the bones.
Well, one must follow an occupation
Somehow if only for a single hour.
So wade half-naked in the yellow water

As though land were bound by a god-vein:
Manacled with mud, then the quick, cold shock
To the genitals as if love sent you
A warning. Still, swimming on in topaz
Diluted by the body's rich, musk philter,
You mean to reach the bank, golden, streaming,
Your brown back rising like a cabochon:
Now a whole strange country is your setting—
If it were not so hot, or had been dusk,
You might have chosen to be Harlequin,
Sleek, dancing on a tessellated floor,
Let a voluptuous woman play your nerves,
A skeleton leap up jingling show tunes—
But it was not the morning for medley.
Perhaps you wanted to flaunt your creamy shoulders,
Perhaps the sun threatened to break a yolk
Over you unless you ran for the water—
I shall analyze these vagaries one
Fine day, trace them to traumas and treatments
So that the music of the zither will
Not come upon me with such sharp frisson,
Hand perhaps a hair shirt to Harlequin.
But let that be I pray quite near the end
As if one gathered the veins of the eyes
Together, bringing in the world at sundown.
Meanwhile, the wetback wins his bright moment,
Arching up the land, a jewel rising:
I see an amber stain in a mirror
As if a spot had traveled from my eye.

## *THE ADDICT*

Autumn now. He lies like a golden stone
Beside the pool. Water has given what it can give.
He had taken knowledge, and been known:
His alter element accepts the way he wants to live.

Moreover, he accepts—a warm, warm, saturated thing
With just a hint of cold impulsion in the blood.
Why should he persist in that embracing fling
Of arms or haunt the diving board with manic thud
Antagonists require, an alien world propelling?

And yet we hope complexities are not in too deep
If that is what occasioned his bright spiral.
The sun would not agree so fully with his sleep
If it thereby withdrew his motive and his moral.
Should the stone quite jettison its griffin?—
He flashed, remember, all wings and tawny torso—
I dream with him, do not begrudge such myths done,
But in the darkness, like a labyrinth, I cannot quite forgo
Preening with a beak once whetted on the sun.

## *THE MISCHIEF IN THE MIRROR*

Following his own sensual footprints, the man went back to the mirror,
More ruddy, sanguine, as he walked, picking up his life and color
Until he stood before that reflecting ovum in which the child of savages is born.

Having retraced the peacock fantail of his steps
So that the muck of iridescence almost would not let him go,
He pulled his feet from heavy sapphire and struck the mirror like a gong.

But it stared at him as if it were a blank, flowed-out face—
Where were his savage parents, the original river and the war canoes,
The gorgeous feathers that were meant to geyser from his head?

Who was that absurd, heavy, and imposing man in business suit
Who acted as if he had just taken off a pair of jeweled leggings,
Safe from his last encounter in a swamp of crocodiles?

I permit myself this fantasy on those days when I feel shod
with turquoise,
And call upon the mirror in my room for such exuberant
retort
As if it were forever pouring out an afterbirth of blue.

The leggings, long gone, and now the dark blue socks,
Keeping only the blue soles for some last flare-up of
incandescence—
I want a brown brave at the moment he set out to spread the
vast pretensions of his tribe.

Lifting the hidden blue sole, a leg that refuses to be anything
but white.
One cannot luxuriate before the milked-out glass—
I stand morose and matte, an eidolon in the dark drab of
stocking feet.

Try it some morning when you are thickly stocked with a heavy
blue life—
Stand naked in your socks, survey the country peacock-linked
around you:
Somewhere the mirror hoards the iris of a deliquescent
waterfall.

The footsteps you retraced have not entirely lied to you—
It is just that forwards and backwards go at very different
speeds:
The brave running in a G-string, the man with all these many
treasures for his tribe.

# IV. *THE TAIL OF THE TOUCAN*

## *SAND HOG*

The man on the suspension bridge may dream
Of being a sand hog, but let me tell
Him this—beware of the dream of the mole,
The desire never to see space again,
One's nerves hung out like a harshly plucked lyre,
Wind-rift and sea gull, the jangled music—
Your eyes can never be truly shut, you
Can never be rid of the river's sound.

What do you think they do beneath the bridge—
Sleep like sleek pigs in a mud paradise,
Their pink skins never to be scorched by sun,
An affluent always floating above,
No care for winding somewhere safe to sea,
The earth's dark, moist depths cored with narcotic?—
I say the sand hog does not savor thus,
Mouth pressed to the cool teat of a pylon.

Settle in air for uncertain music,
Sweat dropping crystal notes in the hard sun.
I know what it is, the minor maggot,
The full world much too big for you to eat,
A vast indigestion when you dig, dig,
The comatose body barely nibbled.
I have seen them come up stuffed with wet sand—
You do not need their weight to make you fall.

## *TWO-WAY STRETCH*

The earth reaching as far as the navel,
While the sky pulls up from the heart—You know
This horizontal and hermaphroditic
Feeling, the thrust of the bulb and balloon.
The old engravings of hermaphrodites
Showed them vertically split down the middle,
One half wanting to walk from the other.
But ours is a much later conception
As if time turns us now upon our sides,
As though gravity wants and rejects us—
We have the lightest feeling among flowers,
Somewhat heavier with the animals,
The belly's bag of lust, the old baton.
Still, one never quite accepts this layered
Creature like the pulled drawer that does not fit
In the right level of the stuffed bureau.
Hence, always the sense of having been robbed,
Scattered possessions in disheveled rooms—
Therefore, I suggest the stereoscope,
The cropped navel and the great floating head,
Close, aligned for a moment in the mind,
Implying a pit in our sentiment
And some soaring in the deep bowel rung:
The feeling of petals in the banked sperm,
The tow on the tail of the bright toucan
When it has bitten too deep in the sky.

## *NUDE INDIGO*

In the nostalgic evening the sun is seldom rude—
After the raw fictions of the day one needs a softened light,
The brilliant white skin turning blue upon a standing nude.

Time which has flashing banners also takes the veil—
The net of twilight settles down into the flesh
Which lifts the small, preceptive bruise upon the half-moon
of a fingernail.

The beautiful blue nude comes forward at this hour
As if she had broken the law, walked through every stop
sign,
And left prostrate in the streets some vivid and exploded
power.

You and I who told so many stories in the acid light,
Rolled the manhole covers down the street like giant, blinded
eyes,
Mean, so we say, to go right on forever fighting in the night.

But at the lowest level of the day something is the matter—
We see the blue light in the window, the white woman
retreating—
Is she the one iconoclasts save for last to shatter?

We will not give in, of course—What then could be the
trouble?—
I look at a vein in the arm, you call for a glass of wine,
And every victory in the world, in that blue nude, is looking
for its double.

## *SWIMMING NEAR THE INTERSTATE*

Steeped in illusion, the water lilies
Could not be mastered by the naked man—
His nerves went out to them like fine gold wire,
But the subjugation of cloisonné,
The suave flattening out of force in the crude
Blue of the water so that he could have

A smooth pavement to walk on were refused—
No use to swear, thrash, and beat the surface.
Nevertheless, with his tight, reeled-in gold,
What was he good for but a jactation?—
You have seen these swimmers swirl in the thick pond
As if to clear a bright place for themselves,
Legs dangling with the long roots of lilies,
Their handsome heads like pads for the Frog Prince—
So it is moving through the thick of things
One learns what underlies the world's pavé:
The wet, glistening head, the scented shoulders,
The hard mind longing for the steamroller,
The flowers' refusal to be cobbled—
I put my hand upon a lily face;
The gold spreads, a flower bobs, the waffling
And buckling in the water promises
To go on forever—nothing put down.
Meanwhile, the cars zoom by, accounting for
Miles and miles of the earth's acquiescence—
How good it is to be nervous and naked,
Turning, turned in a batter of flowers,
The body, the water, entente cordiale—
Someone screeching his tires may stop and stare
As though the road released a pediment,
The risen figure of pure relief.

## *THE WATER HOLE*

The alligator feeding the fat snake into his jaws like rope
With nothing at the other end but the padlock of a head
Looks dangling with distraught desire, yet greedy with hope.

His water holes are drying up, he cannot hate
As lavishly as he once did, as he still would—
He must lie in the sun and live remembering what he once
  ate.

Still, there are men—young, foolhardy wrestlers—so back
into the water.
His first glimpse of those legs, white and juicy as
water-plants,
Gives a fresh, evolutionary twist to the cramped tableau of
slaughter.

The man who may have wrestled many loves to find his own
Will pin down something like a power in himself,
Or feel the saws cut through flesh, firm as hearts of palm,
clean to the bone.

Someone bungles, makes the wrong decision, someone sags—
A hot, thick, antediluvian vein ruptures in the water,
Or a foot floats up, strings of a bloody harp stream from the
flesh in rags.

The tight, reductive, world looks open there for everybody's
stain
Whether we walk radiant, whole, limp on a stump, or swing
an alligator bag upon an arm—
One will pass that way from time to time to dip and dye the
faded hungers of the brain.

## *THE PLETHORA*

So this is the place for the seppuku
By the blue pool where the released entrails
Will wriggle like pink snakes in the water—
I read this sentence in the morning light,
Touching the soft gold of the tanned stomach.
I have alerted myself to violence
As if an old sunset roiled in the gut:
The belly hung like a kangaroo's pouch,
The fistula of enwrapped intestines,

The bland pool utterly taken by surprise—
I knew a man who swabbed his clear, blue eye
With just such an image each bright morning
As if it were the grain in the oyster,
The pip that will look for the pomegranate,
And he must pearl and pearl or plant all day,
Keeping in this secret bag of himself
As though he had swallowed Medusa's head—
Such a man cuts a finger by the pool:
A bandaid closes the bubbling jewel—
It would be too tight and far too much
If he had not stained his sight long before,
The knife flashing like the beak of a bird,
His own hand turning on Prometheus.
You who are the mime of this deep blue
And I, so passionate in parody,
Must be sure of these clear, still mornings,
That they do not crowd sunrise with sunset
And the toyed-with is not so totalized.

## *TOMATOES*

Glowing on the vine, they lure us like incomparable loot,
A skinful of sun ore, carved rubasse hanging in the air,
And yet soft enough to be hurled as Communist fruit.

But for those of us who never plan to be on center stage,
The object of vendetta or admiration now turned sour,
It is enough to slowly watch the green tomato come of age.

It is like watching summer giving birth to some fat jewel.
You would not think the gray-green nodule, homely as a tick,
Harbored the brilliant secret of miscegenation by the sun's
  aggressive fuel.

Shaped full and ripe, it does incite the land—

One can scarcely blame the young bearded anarchist in a bright bandana
For lovingly tucking its loose red wealth into the hollow of his hand.

Who knows? The most timid of us may be come upon in the middle of the square,
Accosted by some wild cry such as "Do you want to live forever?"
And receive, rude as a lover's slap, a red-starred message trickling down the ear.

One could do worse than be so assaulted by soft seed—
There are snowballs cored with rock, cobblestones, Molotov cocktails,
So many ways to make the undiscovered tyrant or unwilling Christ stagger into public view and bleed.

## *THE GRAPNEL*

Sometimes the hand awoke and reached a hook
Into the brilliant and recessive light.
Only yesterday it had played the faun,
Stroking its sensual spots in a lucid mirror,
But what came after the afternoon but night—
The feeling of tweezers, eyelash by eyelash,
Bit by bit, removing the sleek costume,
A whole secret life pulled out by the roots?
Nothing is left but a skullcap for bald Pierrot,
The nightlong flapping of dreams for white sleeves,
One still, black spot, a target over sex.
Is it any wonder that we reach out
As if the arm extended like a crane,
The last magniloquence of Captain Hook:
Ah, ah, ah to the fast-slipping morning,
The hand making a gold egg of the world,
Cracking in, if need be, dripping with yolk,

Hoping that cherubs will light on the prongs,
Resting in pink cameos a sanction of rings.
If, as it pulls away, this casting in
To life falls short, rakes in, and strikes the heart,
You will know that the crane has done its work,
Dropped the reduced egg with infinite care,
And you can pin the arm in its loose sleeve
To the chest where the fallen treasure lies.
We have seen the disguised, dyspeptic faun
Stand on the streetcorner as leaves drift by,
Oblivious of tatters, leave-takings—
He has a delved spot now that will not fade
Nor stick on the lips of any fulsome day.

## *POMADE*

You knew he was there at once—your house his home,
His hair smelling of apples, bringing in the garden,
No head more like Eden's original fruit—the pome.

So fresh you did not need to leave the door ajar—
Just a touch of fragrance here and there among the brilliant
  curls—
You have been driven up the wall by that loud lotion or
  lingering cigar.

Is it the one that does it or the way that it is done?—
We all have friends who crush the pomace, set the pompadour,
Sit too close and are accused of using pomade by the ton.

Open the windows, empty the ashtrays, alert the broom:
Where is the pomander ball that old aunt sent?—
Best of all, bring back the man who brought those apples in the
  room.

In general, thus, I do not hold with scented hair—

Too few have learned just how to start and when to stop,
How much is quite enough to take, pervasive in the air.

If brevity is the soul of wit, the merest scent
Of apples may be even enough of Eden on the head
Which knows, pomaceous to the end, how far down hill the
story went.

## *SPECIAL EFFECTS*

Watching the white tumult on the table
When someone pushes his glass, spills the wine
Like bloodstains moving on the aroused waves,
I loosen the riotous imagination,
Remember the rolls of fat the belt contains,
How we sit always a little with held breath,
How the ring strikes a warning on crystal
And the shuffling feet rumple the carpet.
One finger lies on the damp, ruffled cloth
Like a surfer sprawled, dashed down on his board.
Will that rhinestone necklace slip its chain,
The sprockets drop that woman in the sea?—
In spite of the scented air, we smell salt
In each other, the man in the blue suit
So deeply saturated his smoke rings
Are like mist from the blowhole of a whale.
It is impossible, you say, never
To make waves—the skin itself is always
Moving imperceptibly toward wrinkles,
The drapery bunches in the suave still life,
And the red apple bobs like a buoy.
We ripple on the bed as the heart desires,
The boom, boom, boom until we burst with spray—
No wonder we dress for dinner and eat
With the precision of reformed savages,
Leaving only blood smears, tiny tidbits,

Dosed as we are with the great rolling waves.
The deep fathoms are running in our legs,
Our blue eyes so bright in the new white mask,
Yet still startled when we stagger with drink
As if life meant us all to be artists.
We will not know as we lean together,
Jostling like statues in deepest water,
Just how we trade these footholds in the blue.
But I have found on the lips of a lover
The traces of a bartered triumph,
The fallen column and the fading sea.

## *THE SOFT SPOT*

Ah, you rascal, you with your roses, your women, and your wine,
The pinks and the purples, the passionate sunset on the terrace
Where you invite your latest darling ostensibly to dine.

You light the candles, pour the gorgeous liquid, take her by the arm:
She is the only temptress you have ever really loved
Or so you manage to convey with great aplomb and devilish charm.

Thus nothing in the world for you ever will grow stale:
You put first things first and put them last as well—
No one in their own right mind would know you wear a coat of mail.

Ah, but you do, you rascal, fulgent link and mesh—
Those dawns and sunsets, those arms and arms, those lips and lips
Have hardly left a spot uncovered on your brilliant flesh.

This latest one, does she see you now, silvered, soldered, and a little stark:

The long and rich crusade that hides the purple heart—
Those tender ears—are they aware of just some clanking in the
dark?

The cosseting, the overprinting—how could kisses lie at last so
thick and melded?
That fatal evening when you want to send the metal flying
Someone beautiful and half in love with death imprints the
missing piece that must be welded.

## *BOOMERANG*

The woman tore the topaz from her hand,
Dashed the amber beads upon the table.
At last autumn was over—just like that.
Her lips were still an animal red—the kill,
The slaughter, were finished in field and barn.
A sharp, bright seal in her window would say
A Gold Star mother lived in the cold house,
Thus marking her like the Star of David.
A little later the glass would be steamed,
Her own variant of a gas chamber.
That rich, clinking ring was like the pellet—
How can one admit this extravagance,
This taking of seasons too much to heart
As if the last leaves swooned only for her,
As if buried bullets were the last shot
Of a heavily burdened, jeweled life?
Just this morning, this fabulous woman
Was thrown from my mind like a boomerang,
Harder than crow's wings and much more laden,
In its essence, collapsed, like a bent sword,
Something one wields without any warning,
An image soaring to the edge of things,
Curving, incoming, back to the sender—
One can unfold it now—the golden fan
As if she spread herself like a peacock

To whom the sun has given gilded eyes:
Many pleats, rustlings, the tense hand
Alert to leash the shimmering movement—
Some woman unfazed, no fear of autumn,
Comes into the bright room, and you must hold.
Should she ever pick up the boomerang,
You too will fold into yourself for flight.

## *DREAM POOL*

So it came down to this—the pool and their solarium.
The day might be steeped in minor little horrors wanting to be major:
Slide the glass doors back, and they, in that bright moment, had come home.

Of minorities, you see, they were a race of two,
Unless they counted on the sunlight as a brilliant sister
Or, in a kind of racial greeting, were brothered by that blue.

Woolgathering in the corners stood the tropic plants—
If sun and water were not quite family enough,
In a pinch, perhaps, they might stand in for cousins and for aunts.

No apologies, embarrassment—they meant to save
The world by closing off a flawless square of light:
So they were nude—well, then, it was the plants who must behave.

Save the panda, save the sea lion, save two people in a pool—
One learns a bit each bitter day how hard it is
To be an intermittent student in this sometime saving school.

The pool, the panda, and the sea lion—let them change your mood.
The bumper sticker varies with the moving enclave:
Ah, lovers, Ovid said that two could make a multitude.

# V. *CONCILIUM*

# V. *CONCILIUM*

## *THE KITE*

You will never know how much I counted on the kite,
That inverse parachute so laden with high hopes,
And wondered if my nerves were equal to the flight.

It was a treasure-box, yet open at both ends,
All a mandarin green with black ideographic streaks,
Itself, in part, deception, as though it must discount the
  wind's deceiving trends.

Those deceived too often do two things:
Cut off all intercourse between the earth and sky—
Or make a changing, changeling, philosophy of their
  misgivings:

So doing, they will not give up their least, most fragile, ship,
The jewel-case that long ago has learned to travel light
And balance on the invisible juggler's erratic fingertip.

Someone else who reads the language of the sky
And feels the wind rush through the walls of his resources
Will watch me, brisk as a general, recouping the tension on
  which all spectacles rely.

There is some serenity in knowing that I, at least, will never
  cut the cord.
Both mystery and destruction of an ultimate sort—or so it
  seems to me—
Like falling into heaven, are more appropriate to the Lord.

## *THE BIG BANG IN FLORIDA*

When the questions with their dark hooks oppose
Each other's erratic punctuation
Like two mismatched birds staring off the page,
You can confer with the minimalists,
Throw up a brilliant backdrop of your own—
Floridian sky, green skin of a lake—
And start stalking the absurd flamingos
That lift their feet as if they walked in sludge.
The eyes, bright holes pierced in thin, sharp heads,
Their short-tailed bodies like pink, lifted ducks,
They pause with their interlocking sigmas.
At this point, bring out your own clean, white page—
When armchair philosophers go to work,
Problems besides punctuation glow up.
I have seen many a man fold his screen
Like a fan and go home well before sunset
For milk, crackers, with the minimalists.
But once you have set up opulent scenes,
I believe in lifting words like the feet
Of flamingos, cautious, gingerly,
As if rubescence walks on hidden mines:
A huge, pink puff—and there goes Florida.
You may bring nothing home from holiday
But a pink feather too soft for a quill.
Nevertheless, practice the steps in private,
The lifting, looking about, the stabbed eye—
This failing, promote the exquisite notion
That you can drop the thick mud-shoes at will,
A storm of questions scything in the sky.

## *THE HEAD MASTER*

So all that he had was some flowers and a book,
Heavy, pink oleanders in a blue, figured, Japanese vase—
What would happen to the blossoms if the quiet house
  shook?

The yellow book where the lilac shadow of the flowers
  spread—
Why had they been left to him alone, this spare
  predestination,
Poured as an afterthought on to the table from his head?

Are we given this unusual power to secrete, emit,
Beyond the passions of humanity, some pictorial balm
As if a man could take his head right off his shoulders and
  get rid of it?

That is his head, have no doubt of it, this once at least, for
  now—
After the angers and the oaths that rot the brain like cheese,
He can tilt a bit and take this deep, ironic bow.

He can say to everyone around: I had this in my head as
  well—
If I cannot quite have goddesses to spring from it,
Here is this book, this lilac shadow, these flowers with their
  fragrant smell.

It is all the more remarkable, almost Oriental, this courtesy
  on view,
This bowing, bowing, exquisitely laden, all over the Western
  world,
The totally enchanting and disarming evidence that man can
  make the manners too.

## *THE BLUE HAMMER*

Too much of a white lump of nothing done,
The man wanted to be wrapped in blue foil,
At least a glistening statue for starlight.
They beat silver, he knew, in India
To coat the pill, wrap food or chocolates—
Why not a full integument of blue?
The sky had thickened for just this purpose,
And on the white table the blue hammer
The riveter in himself had laid there:
All those blue-sky buildings and this white lump,
All those mannequins lifted in blue jeans—
The great, incomparable garden of steel,
How had he learned to hang it from the ground?
Now he lies like a rhizome on the couch,
All furry below with sensitive roots.
Brought up, laid bare by narcosynthesis,
He talks of nothing but the blue hammer—
The little more that's left for bright wrapping,
Blue moons on his hands where the nails were struck,
The blowtorch with its violent afterglow,
The immense, far-flung scattering of rivets.
He does not want so much to be rebuilt
As relumed, a white cinder in high sheen—
Count this as one of the lushest vagaries:
The incumbent versus the recumbent
With the whole loose world brooding over him,
The last, strong help a hammer-throw away.
So much for the session, the doctor's quirk
Of keeping mints upon his swept desk—
The blue taste lingers, lingers on the tongue.
You will never be wrapped quite so, one piece
In a pyramid of perpetual pleasure—
What is that heavy noise upon the brain
As if it hammered down into its host
The blue man made of ever-after mints?

## *CRAVING THE POLAR BEAR*

The conflict for some of us is always in the fur—
Softness and pristine purity, in an ideal world,
Should belong to an animal that would nuzzle one's hand
   and purr.

I have always longed for an amenable, yet massive, pet,
A lion or leopard to roam freely through the house
And not, in the midst of a kiss, provide kismet.

Of course, a polar bear would have to be for summer days,
Splashing in some blue imaginary pool beside the house,
Open to touch, endearment, immaculate of predatory ways.

What a comedown if one must settle for a rug,
Dry, as time goes by, and yellow as an old man's beard,
The flat, impoverished ghost of how the heart required an
   all-embracing hug.

*Dura lex sed lex*—At best we settle for the tentative,
Not the gloriously hirsute, an extension and rejection of us
   all:
I will never bring him into the house on a leash—He will
   therefore let me live.

But do not tell me that the house is always radiant and full
As I would have it be. I shall have that rug one day, if all
   goes well,
And sometimes watch glass eyes look up as though I were a
   hanging on the wall.

# *THE CHANNEL SWIMMER*

The man had been told this and that about himself,
That he should use this figure of speech, but not another, walk not waltz,
And sometimes, but only sometimes, he had believed them.

He had been warned that if he swam against the tide
It would leave a stain—as if he were not already covered with oil
And the water could roll over him and print what it wanted.

It was as simple as this—he meant against all odds to swim the channel,
And the sea could be streaked with the babel of extracted and subjected language.
All that really mattered was his own secret headline: I crossed.

He might be exhausted and oil-streaked but he would dance down the street
As if it were a hall of mirrors made of human eyes.
It was not the praise only but the finesse of the thing perceived.

One might understand him better if one thought of a magnificent swan,
Heaped with violets, that carried its burden of fragrance
Without spilling a petal and without a stain on its breast from the turbulent water.

This is indeed an odd figure for the twentieth century
When any sodden and bedraggled fowl can pass as a bird of paradise
And the phoenix merely trashes his nest with his ashes.

But it comes as normally and naturally from the mind of the swimmer

As Athena from the head of Zeus, all of a piece and
unapologetic.
These head-births are, in fact, the fuel of his powerful
stroke.

Somewhere in all of this, as there usually is, there must be
some sex—
No more than a tadpole between his legs perhaps
Or a waterproof fuse that burns down under the surface,
packed with the sperm of Leviathan.

It may be nothing more than being oneself sometimes greasy,
gripped in a substance,
And yet not taking on the fixative of everlasting grime
As the swimmer sheds his oil-suit in the victory shower.

It is nevertheless a magical and majestic trick—
Who of us with two eyes for his resplendent looking glass
Can forget him in his leopard skin of mud splotched by the
water

When he climbs ashore and sets free the fragrant and
fabulous swan?
Perhaps the greatest moment of beauty is just this,
Before he has washed himself with the future and is
unafraid to flaunt the freighted figure.

What is so wrong at last in the glancing look of the
superimposed?—
The swan does not even need to sing when it carries such
fragrance:
I could see it still should I dare to close the clear reflections
of my eyes.

## *THE YOUNG GOAT*

There's no mistaking the evidence: the not yet yellowed coat,
  the soft pink tongue.
Even his smell has not gone totally sour—
You know from the way he leaps and gambols, the goat is
  unquestionably young.

He makes the fetid hill, a rankly tropical regression,
The *mise en scène* for something comically alive.
Given half a chance, he will butt you on your stodgiest
  impression.

He says the weeds upon the hill survive the bottle and the can;
He reminds you of how you loved the earth's mad clutter
Until one morning you looked into the mirror and saw an elder
  statesman—

Rather goatlike if one should add an imaginary beard,
A doctor of sanity almost too sanitized:
When was the last time some girl ogled and you leered?

Still, one cannot go back easily to phlegm and milk.
The young goat has all his passions left to shred,
And you with wise composure must see your pelt acquire some
  yellow in its silk—

With this to remember—It's you, not the young goat, who own
  the hill.
An enormous rumble of stone like the devil's defecation comes
  down—
There, from the ruin of the world, your billy runs while you
  stand still.

## *CALUMET*

Among the strategically placed pillows
Which she had put there to support his head,
The blue and gold silk, the beige ottoman,
The palm trees in their Chinese porcelain,
He had become indeed her love-object.
It was wise she wore a kind of sunset pink,
The morning no time for such a placement
When the rushed, roving body has no glue—
But as evening comes, one does not mind
The faintest, soft touch of mausoleum,
The cool cabana after too much sun,
The first day at home ending your travels,
A dying fall of compleat cadenza—
The woman herself, her own placed object:
The leg to be stroked, lovely cabriole,
The white arm, the breasts with their pink diamonds.
Our senses are meeting in close cabal—
A lighted match looks like a red rocket;
A cigarette explodes the gunpowder:
We draw in even the wars of the world—
Her explored waist rustles a waterfall,
A field of tobacco lurks in his clothes—
You will have your own variant, of course:
The stasis, the distant stamen at rest,
The gazebo where you smoke a peace pipe;
A homing instinct for the chrysalis.
One will do much better next time—
The blue and gold pillows like a thick bed
Of pansies conjure the butterfly swarm:
No country of the heart too fine, too far.

## *THE PICTURE PUZZLE*

If I could draw a map for you—my mountains, sea, lakes—my Italys and Greeces—
Places never been but loved—the desert with its camel—igloo, kayak, Eskimo—
I would show you just how love can put together a thousand exactly fitting pieces.

I, the sensualist, am nomad, do not have a sensual home—
That is, I love the silken tent of rich sensation,
Unfolded, pegged and panoplied, refolded when I roam.

To be exact, and I am most exact with such legendary themes,
I have traveled here and there upon a rift of floating places
And fed with substance, native to the region, legendary dreams.

I have done better. I have brought into my house the bit, the part.
Never gone Pacific—A single pineapple summons that delightful land:
The girl in the sarong, of course, demands that I require a little less from touch, a little more from art.

The thing itself—When possible, I wrap, unwrap the woman—do not underestimate the man.
I merely talk of that accompanying and complementary force
Which makes the ocean when I see it just that much more blue, the desert, visited at last, more tan.

I do not wish to find the dervish done, the flambé guttered out, the dates all pitted—
I want the Chinese courtesan to rise from China with a lavish bowl,
A fingerbowl perhaps, no more, no less, in which the hand already rich with food is graciously admitted.

## *THE PRIME OF PEONIES*

So now, Primus, the peonies again—
Ruffled in the wind like rumps of pink birds,
These abstracts of the one-legged flamingo,
This suggestion that sunlit grass is water,
A feeling that they lighted from somewhere—
Come back to the old lake, these lucent birds,
These fragrant travelers from some thick beyond.
Two of them together make a single bird,
The stalks of their legs green from the water,
The fleece pink as a lustrous dawn-flight of clouds.
Is that what they want to say?—*Qui vive?*
Is that how they come—fictive, in pairs?
You and I, Primus, the sardonic year—
We know a thing or two, we do indeed:
We sit in the white summerhouse and dream,
A skeletal pair, two stalks of something,
Yes, just so, even before they will fade
Filled with the red lesions of departure,
A white bird, uncertain, cruelly halved—
Therefore, my friend, the implacable return,
As if you kept a feather in your pocket,
Or hid somehow a lake around your heart:
The pink foams along the white summerhouse,
The soft air shivers with birds lighting—
Let us sit lightly here, let us relate
Our stories as one views a standing bird,
Our fingers longing for the ruff of flowers.

## *TEXT FOR THE FLOWER CHILDREN*

Let us live where lemons rhyme their yellow,
Where the bluest, most carnal, sea
Conceives, belies, mortality,
The world androgynous of tart and mellow.

A pipe, water in a crystal glass,
Look sacramental in the sun—
Has some little steadfast cult begun
To make its quiet devotions come to pass?

One cheers the sensual horses from the stands,
Blurred as notes of music on the track;
One loves the sweat, the giddy turning of the rack,
Goes home to rinse verbena on the hands,

But not without an odalisque in tow—
It does not seem to us occasion for alarm
If passion should break out in form
And make our colors know they know.

Andantino, monumental, go simplicities—
We dream of women at the bath
Who do not compromise with aftermath
And wipe the future from their glistening knees.

## *WITNESS FOR THE DEFENSE*

Be a cardinal in a forest full of swallows—
The times need it, and, if it is your nature,
You will sustain the chain-reaction that nearly always follows.

Quick wing-motion and you are there yet out of reach.
Even the busiest parliament of fowls cannot condemn you
  wholly:
The court may even be a place where you can teach.

There is some circumstantial evidence, leaf by leaf,
The forest cannot subsist on brown alone—
The so-called criminal was called upon to give an elegant motif.

Perhaps it can all be settled out of court—

No one was really put upon, put down, or murdered
Though that red vitality may, at first, indeed have seemed a
   sharp report.

No one denigrated, no class distinctions overdone—
I do believe a brilliant bird can show us how
We charge the air without resorting to the gun.

Power-politics at every level? No doubt, no doubt, no doubt—
But I would rather be a swallow burnished by red shadow
Than one who put the cardinal to rout.

# VI. *THE WORK OF THE WRENCH*

## *THE GLYPTOGRAPH*

Ah, to be their sometime partisan, to spend one day a week
Carving on jewels, to gather all the loose and idle hours
Into an intense, incised pressure solely directed toward
  intaglio—

The voyager's memory of oceans chambered through an
  aquamarine,
The beautiful nostalgia of many autumns collapsed and
  cubed in topaz,
The violet tones of all your nude scenes captured in an
  amethyst—

Don't forget either the dog's merde on the carpet,
The laundry hamper smelling like the caves of flesh,
The day the stove caught fire from its own incestuous grease.

I suspect for a while you must be secret in your art—
Some lives that touch yours will have a terrible dispersion
And may resent the cryptic, residual ways of
  crystallographers.

If you treat the lover's kiss as if you lanced a ruby,
You may find bloodstains on the pillow in the morning:
Lips bitten will banish the vampire to his misty castle.

Nevertheless, move in and out of your house, gathering
  motes.
It is remarkable what one can do with the brilliant dust of
  one's experience—
Life densely lived trains the master of compaction.

I have seen my furtive brothers collecting powdered gold
everywhere,
For one must also have a setting—loose hairs of a gilded girl,
sunflowers,
The tongues of lilies, the flakes falling from a house on fire.

Ah, comes the end of the week, the reclusive touch of the
settled stone!—
Some, who remain confirmed voluptuaries, cannot cut it;
They will fondle forever their lives in velvet.

I cannot fully convey to you the moment of incision,
The tempered finesse, the controlled shudder of desire's
exactitude,
The point first pressed against the flaccid powers that have
jelled.

One thing more. Don't ever flaunt your carvings—
The week foams and foams, and will foam forever, with the
silt of fractured jewels:
You cannot live without this wash upon your glyptic hand.

## *DEER PARK*

That fig, that nude, that fulsome faun!—He comes
To tell us to eat the fruit, to make love,
To rip the last tight gauze from the facade.
He offers us flesh for fingerpaintings,
The pink marks, the warm, gross pointillism,
The constant pressure of a masterpiece—
There is no doubt at all that we must fill
Ourselves with fig-seed and the felt, soft flesh
Or be a phantom in the dark faubourg—
Some other woman, fruit, figure—the hand
Quivers with the memory of the horn,
At dawn, a hoofprint in the unmade bed,

A smeared stain, a musk of the last mashed kiss.
So the story goes—fruit juice on every page,
Streaked, mingled with the Rorschach of hot tears:
Ladders in the stockings, the rifled tree;
Dangling suspenders, an inept noose;
The tired faun at last let out for the day.
Still, a certain magnificence aspires—
The whole world is shaded with our colors.
One walks plush as if half-loaded with pips;
A fauvist still drinks at the turned faucet,
The red lips pressed like a fruit for filling;
The upturned sole has been inked with crushed grape,
And there through the window, the fresh, young deer
Leap in the park leaving their line drawings
Like clean notations for another night.
One starts with the fig, falters in feeling,
Nibbles exotic perfume in the air,
Takes the mottled painting hand from the glove,
Always your own procedure, touch system.
We will join the others in the meadow,
The luxuriant, sunlit fête champêtre:
The deer are dining on our metaphors.
Be glad that we give them such plump pasture—
No wonder they fatten, move in the house
To tell us what to eat and whom to love.

## *AFTER DEGAS*

Ah, ironist, feeling these days so much ironed out—
The wrinkles are gone, but so are the fruit stains and
  passion:
The soul is a starched, fresh-pressed shirt—no tail to flout.

Over and over the cloth, some damp, forgetful hand,
The colors rising around the laundress as in a Degas
  painting—

How could the fabric, richly marked and drenched, become so bland?

The click of the metal on those pearl, albino eyes—
It sounds like a special, poignant pleading in Morse code:
Going, going up in tinted steam, the bird of paradise.

The helpless man in the shirt, the agonizing stare—
What good does it do to think of his lost, fabulous aura
Or how he, alone, could float such brilliant feathers in the air?

Ironist, suck in, live on, live thinly molded.
Perhaps it is no small thing to have launched an atmosphere,
And feel on some spare days too overbleached, too folded.

Think of the fresh, formal shirt, the absolute, delicious thrill:
Strawberries dipped in confectioner's sugar, the lip running over,
And you can start, with just one spot, a life of iridescent overkill.

## *SLIP OF THE TONGUE*

Certainly one thinks of the remote island,
The rocks deep in guano, the obscene birds—
What is a lady-killer doing here,
With long memories, in tight red loincloth?

The shackled ankles may provide a hint,
The brown body's sprawled, thrown look,
No whip marks, but surely the startled eyes
Wonder if sensation will strike again.

What was the last thing said to the lover?—
Was it a *lapsus linguae* so dreadful

That all the fawning cherubs left the bower
And the woman herself melted like wax?

Sometimes even while they were making love
He could roll over and see the island—
Himself the stripped-down ladrone, the bird mess—
Roll back again and rush the luscious kiss.

It was simply that one night he turned and stuck—
At last she had heard him all too plainly
And with her lips she would not pull him back,
An elastic touch stretched once too often.

Nevertheless, let us taunt sensation,
Make it leak slowly back into the facts:
Why did the lady-killer lose his nerve,
Why did the rushing kiss reverse itself?

I who so love language cannot believe
It alone delivers us to rocks and guano.
Some physical playback jumps the music
And one says what has never been said before.

Ah, lovely flesh—an aesthetic wash
Must roll over it with the passionate kiss—
Two lying at the tropical island's edge:
Just so much tidal thrust, then back again.

Still the eyelid is anchored in nightmare—
Who will be the first to pull, then pull away?—
Sometimes the lucky lie like a lulled ship,
Hung by magic with the deep, plunged iron.

The hot, stifled lungs wanting to be wings,
I wish I could summon Prometheus—
How did the liver grow and live so long,
What was the word the vulture longed to hear?

It is so warm—roll over and roll back,
An exquisite cradle of creation:

I will stick out my tongue to the black bird—
So much for saying something for a god.

## *BLUE SNAPPER BLUES*

It has mainly been the red and silver that I choose.
In the fish shop there they were, flamboyant, argentine—
Quite some time before I knew there was a fish that had the
  blues.

It had its reasons, dead and nestled on the ice,
But then the brothers that I knew had felt the cold for years,
Lying perfectly serene in preparation for a death that
  happened twice.

In the water, on the plate, what matters one more way to die?—
Every time I find an alien point of view pointed at my chest,
I feel it pulling back until it brings about the slightest
  hemorrhage in the eye.

Later, when we sit together beneath a café awning in the dying
  sun,
The hook by then may very well have been removed,
But, red in anger, silver in defeat, I sense that I am being dined
  upon.

In the seafood place the waiter hovers, deferential to my
  wish—
Not so awfully long ago I said to him: So much red and silver—
I think the color will be blue this evening for my fish.

Among congenial friends the former colors will abide,
But every magister of points of view must learn
The first surprise of something come upon already blue before
  it died.

## *IMAGO*

The body had bloomed like a butterfly—
Who would have thought the caterpillar could?
He was so soft and white—Punch or mash him,
A yellow creme would come out on the hands,
The noxious stuff of such involution—
But now he stands at the edge of the pool,
Arms spread like wings cleaned of integument
To be lifted in shawls of shimmering blue.
One has discussed with the posh psychiatrist
The ideal construct, how the fat worm waits
In the heart for the iridescent mantle,
Hiding a tight thread of gold to be spun—
You can see them at the cocktail parties,
Wanting to be drawn out, unspooled, spread fine:
The ritual amber drink, the curled blue smoke,
Offering you ingredients and pigment—
One woman crosses her long silken legs
And you could swear a cocoon is stirring;
The man garroted in a yellow tie
Negotiates for metamorphosis.
Outside, the pool, the released icon:
The exact form separated from mind,
Rising, falling, fluttering in the water,
Extricable in the blue impasto,
Trailing, like thinner, a trace of silver—
Instinct somehow left a window open,
And the fumes and the thick smoke poured out.
To find in full view the naked concept's
Uncurdled fill, the figure, blue and gold,
Explains, confrère, why we swarm together.

# *THE FAN*

When folded, it shows the picture of a man
Because a woman owns it and wants to designate her love:
It seems boldly, exclusively, hermetically, a phallic fan.

Lovers of ambiguity are satisfied without detail—
They do not need to know if rich landscape flows out from
  him,
Or a brilliant, opulent sea from which a ship on ivory sets sail.

That is, they would rather supply and not be told—
For all they know, and they could provide dimensions,
There may be a belly dancer shimmying out and out, fold from
  fold.

These people, and they could be just the very lucky ones,
Are themselves pleated with many strange and foreign affairs,
Crammed with mountains, glaciers, men on horseback, camels,
  dulcet northern, blazing tropic, suns.

Still, the woman must unfold—you know, you know, she will
Much as if, in this, she were a peacock androgyne,
And cannot hold, too long, the shimmering motion of her
  spirit still.

I side and side, and do not always side, with Mallarmé—
Sometimes I stand and stand, let the woman picture me,
  untold, obscure forever,
Then want to see on *eventail,* that spreading arc, a scene, less
  pure perhaps, more spacious of my full array.

## *THE LINCHPIN*

Somewhere at imagination's far edge,
The perfect place, object, of arousal,
The rich lieu where nerves come home to die,
So that a ripe pear sitting in the sun
Promises the ultimate thrombosis—
Ah, at last, tongue says, as the juice goes down
And the hard rondure clears from the bloodstream.
The palm trees are full of executions,
A lush nude going into her spasm,
The opulent somatic oasis
Making the mouth run with suppressed water.
How much of this is buried in almost
Everything we do, a tense gravity
In our entrails pulling at the rainbow,
Wanting that great gate for entrance, exit,
Our best moods always full of tropic rain?
We have seen them coming back from edges:
The man with the briefcase crammed with folded maps,
Women tinting up, down, the face's fruit,
A child with bloody smears of jam on hands
As if palms dripped their gory tale on him—
Some days the cook is a conquistador:
Battlements of meat, mousse, ravishment and rout—
We need a philosopher, indeed we do,
Someone who comes back from the end of things,
Odysseys of sensation winding down,
Courtesans of wax, pears of marzipan,
To bleed a bit those secret, jagged places
Which could not move their iridescent saw.

# *THE BOUTONNIÈRE*

The man may be wilted inside his shirt, the flower not—
It must look as though it were cut daily for his finest hour
Before that hour, going down to mud and blood, should show a
single spot.

A magician's flower that sprays water will not do:
It must be firm as crystal fed by a nerve of fragrance,
A third eye of the third world, looking straight at you.

His own eyes may be shifty, but this one sees you plain—
If you should disappear behind a shirt, the matted,
sweat-soaked hair,
You want a line of vision that can see you home again.

We do not have long moments in the cutting room of finest
hours:
I choose carnations for their spice, you choose a Nehru rose,
And keep the spatted, spastic governments of the world
uncertain of their powers.

Just when the wrinkled blanket of peoples looks dusty, loses
sheen,
And we think we will die in the night from suffocation of the
stippled self,
The man with the boutonnière comes crisply on the scene.

Do not think, my dear competitor, time will not take you by the
throat,
But you will go down more gladly, I suspect, if you can say:
With my two eyes to those three eyes I give a special kind of
vote.

## *A MIRROR FOR BEDOUINS*

Now the rich morning needs its telamon,
The laurel and weigela, pink, maroon—
Now the body must assume the burden
As if every scene rested on its head
And shoulders, the great image Atlased there—
It is a fast sinking world otherwise,
Any garden a quick place of ruins,
Those illusions of pink and reddish stone—
Moreover, the man in his pajamas
Is a willing mummy and only wakes
Wishing not to be unwound, stripped and oiled,
Back-sore with pictorial ambitions,
The white shirt ending in a winding cloth—
Thus this fantasy of image-bearers
Is repressed as an endless caravan
Which carries our lives into the desert—
A little water, some saddlebags
Of colored silk like the skins of flowers:
The pause is much too tense and structural;
One must kneel down, one must remember, pray—
Most mornings, loose, lax, and Oriental,
We stuff the coarse bags with this pot-pourri
And there will be no cities on the plains.
But some days, pitiless in the mirror,
One sees the stripped, uncertain architect
With all those blueprints buried in his veins.
Telamon, telamon, I bend, I boost—
To carry the light world as though it were stone
Will sink the restless nomad in the sand
And let the lichen spread upon the leg.

## *THE HOLLOW OF THE DEEP SEA WAVE OFF THE COAST OF KANAGAWA*

Life vacillates between what we would throw away and save,
What we would discard, jettison, or keep forever—
I got this view of life dreaming that I stood beneath Hokusai's
great blue wave.

In a boat, of course, with just my final hoard—
A book on battles, one on love, another of pressed flowers,
Misted, damp with foam—I would not throw them overboard.

It seemed enough to dream on, love and war and grace—
The huge wave flattened, rose again, hollowed out,
And brought each time its overhanging cliff of water closer to
my face.

I was always on the point of being given one last chance—
Would the book of beauty be the one, or love, or war?—
The wave held out its many hands of spray to my last glance.

You in the meadows, you with your lambs and crook,
Keeping this one and not that one from the wolf, the river, the
abyss,
Know a little of the vision that I had, the boat turned over, the
hand held high, the book.

One feels oppressed, compressed—a choice is made but has no
wings—
The book is closed and will not flutter from the hand:
Two books, or more, were given to the blue surrounding sea,
the unity of things.

# *CLOUD PICTURES*

At sunset, the red clouds lay together
Like lovers fleecy and brilliant with desire.
I hung them, wanted them there forever—
At least this much ardor left in the world.
So stuffed, curdled with the longing to love,
If you have ever watched cirrus passing—
His head hidden in the swaying glitter,
Her body rifted in the stretched-out glow—
You have become a cavalier of clouds.
Therefore, it is no small thing to assume
That something in you will find its image,
That earth answers a little in this way:
A passing cloud caught in some fine glory,
An evening with your own rouged revelers—
Oh, I will pick up the pickaxe tomorrow,
Penetrate, hit rock, chop to the roots,
Leave the blood of flowers on a black stone,
Staggering when the chisel hits my boot,
My muscles twisting the rope of desire,
Tighter, tighter, ready to spring, to rise
To the soft snake-dance music of evening,
The gold nerves still glowing from exertion,
A man wanting to be lit like a torch-end—
So there it is, a projected passion.
Nothing will come of it but itself,
A secret album of such nephograms,
The pickaxe always waiting in the shed,
The lovers on their far, golden mountain.
It is the most exquisite synergy,
This delving and this daring after love—
I lean on the pickaxe and wait for dusk,
So braided and so born to breach a cloud.

## *THE PROMPTER*

With coffee, brandy, cigars glowing at their ends,
It is time to draw down the curtain of the stars,
And, in a little final act of drama, bless the day and make
  amends.

Life may not be a courtyard garden of peace and parasol:
The pink canvas, the lovely flowers, the flagstone terrace,
A fearless, fragrant bonhomie spreading over all.

And yet how long have meals been finished with dessert,
How long have cigarettes, cigars, been lighted, brandy
  poured?—
The end of twilight is a poultice we apply to any hurt.

The leisure, linkage at the table, are a truce with passion that
  incites—
You signal just a little with your hand, I flash back:
Let the fates make what they will of it, this language of cross
  lights.

Of course, a demon hovers, and yet a daemon speaks—
Every evening finds you going toward the courtyard and those
  pink umbrellas:
Even from afar you have their bloom upon your cheeks.

Not that you do not need to watch with care the smallest step
  you make—
Clouds are changing scenes along the river, a mist is toying with
  the stars,
And you can miss the cue of all content with every breath you
  take.

# *THE WRENCH*

The blue pool, golden bodies, pink fruit ice,
The eyes in the pool's rim of peacock tiles—
Something random like a wrench lying there
As if the whole scene had been tuned, tightened:
The blue tympanum laid down by gold screws,
The body bolts beautifully adjusted,
The syrup stirred with steel before freezing—
One could stick a long hatpin in the pool
And it would not wince, rub the gold swimmers
And they would not flake. The fruit ice sits in
Its mound with the poise of a pink iceberg;
The tongue longs to offer it white water.
But the wrench has turned beneath the table:
The lacquered knees, the hidden pagodas,
A cool pink island lifted from the blue.
One does not plunge the spoon until a signal
Is flashed to us perhaps by heliogram:
That sunlight, that bougainvillea shudder!
I mean to come here one day when the parts
Are lying all about, loose, untended,
Look at the still, lonesome teeth of the wrench,
The hiatus between its unfilled lips,
And feel I am reading a hard-core life.
It would be thrilling to hear the first gold turn,
To be one of the first to be tightened,
To sing with the pool as the song stretches
And transfer a peacock eye to my chest—
I would like to be the last with the fruit ice
As though my tongue licked a cold volcano.
If it is not too much to ask, spare me
The tense pleasure of waiting for fireworks,
The tremor that builds in the pagodas
As if lovers learn the sigh of the wrench.